THE JOY OF *Serving*

A 4-week course to help
senior highers discover
the joy of being a servant

by Karen Ceckowski

Group®
Loveland, Colorado

The Joy of Serving

Credits
Edited by Stephen Parolini
Cover designed by Jill Bendykowski and DeWain Stoll
Interior designed by Judy Atwood Bienick and Jan Aufdemberge
Illustrations by Raymond Medici
Cover photo by Brenda Rundback and David Priest
Photos on p. 4, 17 and 33 by Brenda Rundback

ISBN 1-55945-210-2
Printed in the United States of America

CONTENTS

THE JOY OF SERVING

"I've learned that when you serve others, it brings a lot of joy into your heart."

"When you serve others, you can feel God more in your life."

"By serving, we grew in Christ's love and in love for each other."

"The neatest thing I've seen is how God has touched my own group. Some kids were quite selfish at the start, and now they're so willing to care for each other and share with each other. They're looking out for each other."

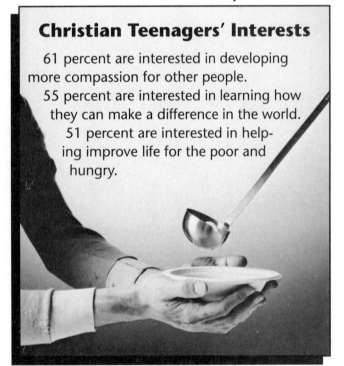

Christian Teenagers' Interests

61 percent are interested in developing more compassion for other people.

55 percent are interested in learning how they can make a difference in the world.

51 percent are interested in helping improve life for the poor and hungry.

These comments by teenagers and youth leaders reflect a sense of wonder at the world of servanthood. Yet in today's society, many teenagers live for what they can *get* from others rather than what they can *give*.

When kids get involved in serving others, they're changed for life. A study of ninth-graders found that involvement in service projects may help improve grades and decrease school discipline problems. The study goes on to say that encouraging teenagers to take on more responsibilities can help develop better relationships between kids and adults.

Teenagers' understanding of what it means to be a servant is likely incomplete, however. While most teenagers are aware of the responsibilities associated with being a waiter or waitress, many don't understand the implications of a lifestyle of servanthood—as modeled by Jesus.

The church can help. When teenagers reach out to serve others, they begin to understand the big picture of servanthood. And when they read about Jesus' life of serving, they realize the importance of serving others.

One of the biggest trends in the '90s will be for teenagers to focus on contemporary needs. After the "years of excess" in the '80s, kids are ready for a decade of servanthood. This course will help your teenagers learn to take part in that national focus on serving others. It'll help them discover how to walk in Jesus' humble footsteps. And it'll help them understand what Paul says in Ephesians 2:10: "For we are God's workmanship, created in Christ Jesus to do good works, which God prepared in advance for us to do."

By the end of this course your students will:
● know the qualities of a servant;
● explore biblical examples of servanthood;
● explore what it means to be a suffering servant, according to Jesus' example;
● develop and follow through on service projects for family, friends and others;
● identify their neighbors and determine ways to help them; and
● encourage servant attitudes.

COURSE OBJECTIVES

HOW TO USE THIS COURSE

Think back on an important lesson you've learned in life. Did you learn it from reading about it? from hearing about it? from something you experienced? Chances are, the most important lessons you've learned came from something you experienced. That's what active learning is—learning by doing. And active learning is a key element in Group's Active Bible Curriculum.

Active learning leads students in doing things that help them understand important principles, messages and ideas. It's a discovery process that helps kids internalize what they learn.

Each lesson section in Group's Active Bible Curriculum plays an important part in active learning:

The **Opener** involves kids in the topic in fun and unusual ways.

The **Action and Reflection** includes an experience designed to evoke specific feelings in the students. This section also processes those feelings through "How did you feel?" questions and applies the message to situations kids face.

The **Bible Application** actively connects the topic with the Bible. It helps kids see how the Bible is relevant to the situations they face.

The **Commitment** helps students internalize the Bible's message and commit to make changes in their lives.

The **Closing** funnels the lesson's message into a time of creative reflection and prayer.

When you put all the sections together, you get a lesson that's fun to teach—and kids get messages they'll remember.

● Read the Introduction, the Course Objectives and This Course at a Glance.

● Decide how you'll publicize the course using the art on the Publicity Page (p. 9). Prepare fliers, newsletter articles and posters as needed.

● Look at the Bonus Ideas (p. 43) and decide which ones you'll use.

● Read the opening statements, Objectives and Bible Basis for the lesson. The Bible Basis shows how specific passages relate to senior highers today.

● Choose which Opener and Closing options to use. Each is appropriate for a different kind of group. The first option is often more active.

● Gather necessary supplies from This Lesson at a Glance.

● Read each section of the lesson. Adjust where necessary for your class size and meeting room.

● The approximate minutes listed give you an idea of how long each activity will take. Each lesson is designed to take 35 to 60 minutes. Shorten or lengthen activities as needed to fit your group.

● If you see you're going to have extra time, do an activity or two from the "If You Still Have Time . . ." box or from the Bonus Ideas (p. 43).

● Dive into the activities with the kids. Don't be a spectator. The lesson will be more successful and rewarding to both you and your students.

● The answers given after discussion questions are responses your students *might* give. They aren't the only answers or the "right" answers. If needed, use them to spark discussion. Kids won't always say what you wish they'd say. That's why some of the responses given are negative or controversial. If someone responds negatively, don't be shocked. Accept the person, and use the opportunity to explore other angles of the issue.

THIS COURSE AT A GLANCE

Before you dive into the lessons, familiarize yourself with each lesson aim. Then read the scripture passages.
- Study them as a background to the lessons.
- Use them as a basis for your personal devotions.
- Think about how they relate to kids' circumstances today.

LESSON 1: WELCOME TO SERVANTHOOD

Lesson Aim: To help senior highers identify the qualities of a servant.

Bible Basis: Matthew 20:20-28; Matthew 27:32; and Luke 10:38-42.

LESSON 2: THE SUFFERING SERVANT

Lesson Aim: To help senior highers understand that being a servant sometimes involves sacrifice.

Bible Basis: Isaiah 53:1-5 and Luke 6:17-38.

LESSON 3: SERVING FAMILY AND FRIENDS

Lesson Aim: To help senior highers discover ways to serve family and friends.

Bible Basis: John 13:3-6 and 1 John 3:17-18.

LESSON 4: SERVING THE WORLD

Lesson Aim: To help senior highers find ways to serve their neighbors around the world.

Bible Basis: Luke 9:10-17 and Luke 10:25-37.

PUBLICITY PAGE

Grab your senior highers' attention! Copy this page, then cut and paste the art of your choice in your church bulletin or newsletter to advertise this course on servanthood. Or copy and use the ready-made flier as a bulletin insert. Permission to photocopy this clip art is granted for local church use.

Splash this art on posters, fliers or even post-cards! Just add the vital details: the date and time the course begins, and where you'll meet.

It's that simple.

THE JOY OF *Serving*

THE JOY OF *Serving*

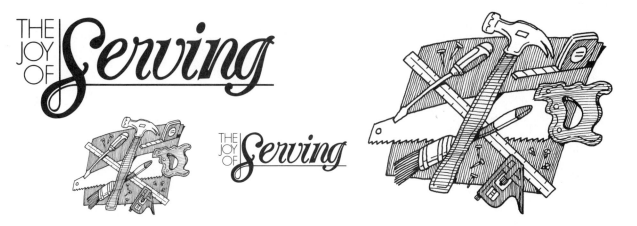

THE JOY of SERVING

A 4-week high school course on what it means to be a servant

Come to _____

On _____

At _____

Come learn how to enjoy serving others!

WELCOME TO SERVANTHOOD

W hat does it mean to be a servant? Many teenagers, when they hear the word "servant," immediately think of a "lowly" or "second-class" person. What they don't realize is the incredible strength of character it takes to be a true servant.

To help senior highers identify the qualities of a servant.

Students will:
● role-play seeking jobs as servants;
● brainstorm the qualities of a servant;
● explore scriptures depicting servants in action; and
● celebrate the servant qualities they have.

Look up the following scriptures. Then read the background paragraphs to see how the passages relate to your senior highers.

In **Matthew 20:20-28**, Jesus explains that whoever wishes to be great must become a servant.

Jesus tells his disciples in no uncertain terms that he didn't come to be served—but to serve. That was an important, humbling lesson for Jesus' disciples to hear. Jesus wanted his disciples to clearly understand that serving others was God's way.

Teenagers are often pressed to be "the greatest" in sports, school and other activities. They, like the disciples, need to understand the importance of becoming a servant.

In **Matthew 27:32**, a man from Cyrene carries Jesus' cross.

Jesus was weakened by the torture he'd been subjected to. So Simon, a man from Cyrene, was enlisted to carry the crossbeam of Jesus' cross to Golgotha. In this way, Simon served both the Roman soldiers and Jesus, since Jesus couldn't carry the cross himself.

In many ways, Simon's act of serving—whether by choice or not—is an example of how teenagers should serve Jesus in any way they can. And it also shows that serving can sometimes be difficult.

THIS LESSON AT A GLANCE

Section	Minutes	What Students Will Do	Supplies
Opener (Option 1)	up to 5	**Check Your Time**—Define what they do with their time during the week.	Paper, pencils
(Option 2)		**Service**—Find magazine pictures depicting services and discuss what service means.	Magazines
Action and Reflection	15 to 20	**Now Hiring: Servants**—Role-play interviewing for jobs as servants.	"Job List" handouts (p. 17), markers, newsprint
Bible Application	10 to 15	**Scripture Servants**—Explore what the Bible says about serving.	Bibles, serving platters or paper plates, 3×5 cards, pencils, cookies
Commitment	10 to 15	**Servant Qualities**—Complete a handout and talk about being servants.	"Now Hiring" handouts (p. 18), pencils
Closing (Option 1)	up to 5	**Good and Faithful Servants**—Tell which servant qualities others have.	
(Option 2)		**Two Servants**—Determine what kind of servants they are.	Bible

The Lesson

OPENER
(up to 5 minutes)

☐ OPTION 1: CHECK YOUR TIME

Give kids each a sheet of paper and a pencil. Have students each list their typical week's activities. Have kids list everything they do in a week based on the time they spend doing each activity. Have kids account for every hour. Remind kids there are a total of 168 hours in a week. For example, someone might write, "In one week I spend 30 hours in school, 10 hours doing homework, one hour in church, two hours at a youth group meeting, six hours on the phone with friends, 15 hours eating, 35 hours watching television, two hours cruising, four hours with my boyfriend, 62 hours sleeping and one hour talking with my parents."

Once the lists are complete, explain that one end of the room represents zero hours and the other end of the room represents 168 hours (or the entire week).

Ask students to stand in the area of the room representing the number of hours they spent doing each of the following things:
- Going to school
- Sleeping
- Eating
- Watching television
- Attending church or youth group activities
- Doing things for yourself
- Doing something for someone else

Then ask:

● **What surprised you most about the responses?** (Lots of people watch television all the time; not much time is spent at church.)

● **What surprised you least about the responses?** (We all like to sleep and eat; we do a lot for ourselves.)

● **What'd you notice about the number of hours people spent doing things for others?** (People didn't spend much time doing things for others; people were generous with their time.)

Say: **It's good for us to think about how we spend our time. We can discover how much we do to help ourselves and how much we do to help others. Helping others is the focus of this course. If you had a hard time thinking of things you did for others, this course will help you begin thinking like a servant. If you already enjoy helping others, this course will help you refine your servant skills.**

☐ OPTION 2: SERVICE

Bring out a stack of magazines. Have students sit in a circle, thumb through the magazines and find an ad depicting services. Go around the circle, and have people each tell about the services offered by their ad. For example, a credit card ad may offer convenience, simplicity and prestige.

Once kids have each shared an idea, ask:

● **Would these services cause you to use the items? Explain.** (Yes, convenience is important to me; no, I don't need the prestige.)

● **When you hear the words "service" or "serving," what first comes to mind?** (Serving others; getting waited on at restaurants.)

Say: **The word "service" means a lot of different things. We may think of service as something offered to us to make our lives easier. But the service we're going to talk about in this course isn't something to make our lives easier—it's something that may actually make our lives more complicated. We're going to learn about servant-hood and how we can be servants to others.**

NOW HIRING: SERVANTS

Form two groups for a role-playing activity. One group, of no more than six kids, will be Seekers—the people who've placed want ads for help in service-oriented work. They'll be interviewing the Applicants.

The other kids will be answering ads for the jobs. This group will be the Applicants.

Take the Seekers aside. Tell them if the applicants ask how much money they'll be making, to say, "You'll be paid what you're worth." Tell Seekers to never quote a salary or make any promises of what they're willing to give in return for the Applicants' work.

Let the Applicants know they really need to sell themselves. They each need to convince the Seekers that they're the best qualified person for the job.

Give kids each a copy of the "Job List" handout (p. 17).

Assign at least one Applicant to each job. Assign a Seeker to interview Applicants for each job. If you have a large group, you may have more than one Applicant for each job.

Decide on a time limit per interview in order to fit this activity into 20 minutes.

Set up two chairs in the front of the room. Call up a Seeker first and have him or her read the ad he or she is interviewing Applicants for. Have Applicants interviewing for that job come up one at a time and interview for the job in front of the whole class. Once all Applicants for that job have been interviewed, move on to the next Seeker and repeat the process.

After all the interviews are finished, announce that Applicants each have gotten the jobs they interviewed for. Pause to allow kids to congratulate each other. Then say: **However, none of these jobs pays any kind of salary. You'll be working for free.**

Ask the Applicants:

● **How'd you feel as you applied for the jobs?** (Uncomfortable; confident; confused.)

● **How is that like the feeling people have when they do things for others?** (People are uncomfortable helping others; some people are very confident helping others.)

● **How'd you feel when you got the job?** (Great; it didn't seem fair that we all got the jobs we wanted; I felt nervous, I didn't really want the job.)

● **How'd you feel when I said you wouldn't be paid for your work?** (Angry; confused.)

● **Does serving others always have a reward? Explain.** (Yes, the reward is feeling good about yourself; no, sometimes you don't get anything in return.)

Have kids brainstorm qualities that were needed for the jobs advertised. Have a volunteer write these qualities on a sheet of newsprint. For example, the doctor needs to be available at all times for emergencies, so you might write the word "available," or the nurse may need to be understanding.

Say: **As you look at these qualities, think about which you do well and which you don't. During the next few weeks we'll help you find ways to develop the qualities of a good servant. But first, let's take a look at what the Bible has to say about being a servant.**

SCRIPTURE SERVANTS

Form groups of no more than five. Give groups each a Bible, and have them read these scripture passages: Matthew 20:25-28; 27:32; Galatians 5:13-14; and Colossians 3:12-14.

Give groups each a serving platter or paper plate, 3×5 cards, pencils and cookies. Say: **In your groups, discuss what these verses say about being a servant. Write your observations each on separate 3×5 cards. Then place a cookie on each card, and place the cards on the platter.**

After groups have filled their platters with cards and cookies, have them go around the room, serving each other a cookie and card. As they serve the cookies, have them read the card to the person they're serving.

Ask:

● **How'd you feel as you served the cookies?** (It was fun; uncomfortable.)

● **How'd the observations from the Bible match with the qualities we wrote earlier on the newsprint?** (The qualities of servanthood in the Bible were the same as the ones we wrote; the Bible's view of servanthood is broader than what we described on the newsprint.)

● **How can scripture help you be a better servant?** (Show me good examples to follow; remind me of what it means to serve.)

Say: **The Bible is the best handbook for understanding servanthood. From the Bible, we can learn how Jesus was the ultimate servant. And we can learn how to develop the same servant qualities Jesus had.**

SERVANT QUALITIES

Give kids each a "Now Hiring" handout (p. 18) and a pencil. Referring to the list of qualities created in the Now Hiring: Servants activity, have kids complete the handout. Then form pairs. Have partners each share how they completed their handout and discuss the questions at the bottom.

Have kids each promise their partner they'll work on developing at least one servant quality during the coming week. Have kids be specific about what they'll do. For example, someone might say, "I'll work on being more caring by listening to my friends more" or "I'll work on patience by thinking before I act."

BIBLE APPLICATION
(10 to 15 minutes)

COMMITMENT
(10 to 15 minutes)

Table Talk

The Table Talk activity in this course helps senior highers discuss with their parents what it means to be a servant.

If you choose to use the Table Talk activity, this is a good time to show students the "Table Talk" handout (p. 19). Ask them to spend time with their parents completing it.

Before kids leave, give them each the "Table Talk" handout to take home, or tell them you'll be sending it to their parents.

Or use the Table Talk idea found in the Bonus Ideas (p. 44) for a meeting based on the handout.

CLOSING
(up to 5 minutes)

☐ OPTION 1: GOOD AND FAITHFUL SERVANTS

Have kids stand in a circle. Ask students each to think about one quality the person on their right has that makes him or her a good servant; for example: available, good listener, patient, sincere.

Go around the circle and have each person tell the quality they see in the person on their right. Remind kids to be positive and sincere.

Close by saying: **As you can see, each one of us has been given special qualities that enable us to be servants. Together, we can learn to be strong even when serving isn't easy.**

☐ OPTION 2: TWO SERVANTS

Read aloud Luke 10:38-42. Discuss the qualities that Mary and Martha each had as a servant. For example, Martha was good at getting a task done and was a very active servant; Mary was a good listener and made people feel important by listening.

Have kids form two groups based on whether their style of serving is more like Mary's or Martha's. Then have groups each form a circle. Within their groups, have kids each take a turn standing in the center of the circle while others call out reasons they're good servants. Be sure everyone gets a chance to be in the center. Remind kids to be sincere and positive with their comments.

Close by having volunteers in each group pray, thanking God for the model of servanthood he's given us in Jesus Christ.

If You Still Have Time . . .

Serving Stories—Have people who work in serving roles (waiter, sales clerk, babysitter) talk about how they feel when they help others. Discuss how servanthood can be both exhilarating and humbling.
Servant Search—Give kids each a Bible. Have them race to find examples of Bible characters who were servants to others. Then have kids list qualities these biblical servants had. To get kids started, have them look for stories involving David, Moses, Abraham, Jacob, Samuel, Solomon or Jesus.

JOB LIST

Wanted:
Full-time doctor needed for small town.

Wanted:
Wealthy family with two children is looking for a butler to perform various jobs around the house.

Wanted:
Grocery-store bagger needed. Flexible hours.

Wanted:
Full-service gas station needs gas attendant for busy weekend shift.

Wanted:
Hospital in need of nurses for children's ward.

Wanted:
Elderly couple seeks help around the house.

Role-Playing Hints

Applicants: Do your best to convince the interviewers you're the best person for the job. You might want to quote experience, skills and training you've had that would make you the best person for the job. Also, try to find out as much as possible about the job you're interviewing for.

Seekers: In the interviews, ask questions such as:
- Why do you want this job?
- What qualifies you for this job?
- What experience do you have in this area?
- How do you feel about serving others?
- How would your former employers describe your servant attitude?

NOW HIRING

Use the list of servant qualities from the Now Hiring: Servants activity to complete this handout. Then form pairs and discuss the questions at the bottom of the page with your partner.

Servant Opportunities:

Openings for a limitless number of _____ workers to serve the community. Looking for applicants with _____ personality.

Must be willing to _____ for weeks at a time. Previous experience must include _____ and _____.

References required. Apply only if you're willing to _____.

● How would you respond to a classified ad such as the one you just wrote?
● Why do people want to serve others?
● Why do people avoid serving others?
● How can you be a servant to your partner before the end of the day? Decide something you'll do to serve your partner. Then follow through with it before the end of the day.

Table Talk

To the Parent: We're involved in a senior high course at church called *The Joy of Serving*. Students are exploring what it means to be a servant. We'd like you and your teenager to spend some time discussing this important topic. Use this "Table Talk" page to help you do that.

Parent

Complete the following sentences:

● When I think of servanthood, I think of . . .
● As a teenager, an example of servanthood I witnessed was . . .
● One way I serve you is . . .
● One way you serve me is . . .
● My parents served me when . . .

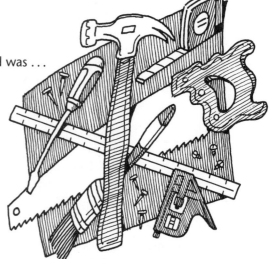

Senior higher

Complete the following sentences:

● Some things I've done to serve others include . . .
● I've served family members by . . .
● One way you serve me is . . .
● One way I serve you is . . .

Parent and senior higher

Talk about the sacrifices people must make to serve others. How does sacrifice make you feel? Tell each other about sacrifices you've made for others. After each story of sacrifice, affirm each other with positive words such as "I appreciate your sacrifice" or "God must smile on your willingness to give."

Tell about:

● a time you served someone and it didn't turn out like you expected.
● how it felt to receive service from someone else.
● what your family life would be like if you were serving others as a missionary in a poor country.

Together, brainstorm ways you can work together on a service project to help others. Perhaps you'll plan a surprise dinner for a relative or "adopt" a nursing home resident.

Identify which of the following servant qualities you see in each other (be specific and explain why you chose each quality): availability; concern for others; sensitivity; patience; leadership; humility; unconditional love.

Read aloud Galatians 5:22-23 together. Talk about how these qualities also make you a good servant. Pray together to be given the hearts of servants.

LESSON 2

THE SUFFERING SERVANT

Serving others isn't always easy. Sometimes it requires sacrifice. Teenagers need to get beyond the idea that servanthood is simply charity or doing nice things. They need to understand the positive and negative implications of following in Christ's footsteps as a servant.

LESSON AIM

To help senior highers understand that being a servant sometimes involves sacrifice.

OBJECTIVES

Students will:
- identify the risks Jesus took to serve others;
- examine how serving others sometimes involves risk or discomfort;
- reflect on times when they felt the cost of serving others seemed too great; and
- encourage each other to serve others in spite of the risks involved.

BIBLE BASIS
ISAIAH 53:1-5
LUKE 6:17-38

Look up the following scriptures. Then read the background paragraphs to see how the passages relate to your senior highers.

Isaiah 53:1-5 describes the coming Messiah as a suffering servant.

In this passage, the author paints a picture of the Messiah that may have surprised the people of his time. The Jews expected the Messiah to be a great king, born of high stature and honored by all. Isaiah paints a much darker picture of the Messiah as a servant who is rejected by many.

The prophet Isaiah knew Jesus would be a servant—not a king according to earthly standards. Teenagers can learn from this passage that serving is better than reaching for earthly goals.

In **Luke 6:17-38**, Jesus describes characteristics of true disciples.

In this passage, Jesus teaches the importance of being humble and loving enemies as well as neighbors. He makes it clear that being a disciple isn't always easy. Yet in spite of the trials, there's great joy in serving.

When teenagers experience the pain or frustration of serving others, they often get discouraged. This passage can remind them that they can have joy in the midst of difficult times.

THIS LESSON AT A GLANCE

Section	Minutes	What Students Will Do	Supplies
Opener (Option 1)	5 to 10	**Serving Reflections**—Describe times they've served others.	Large mirror
(Option 2)		**Servant Risks**—Discuss and experience risks of servanthood.	Newsprint, markers, paper cups, water
Action and Reflection	10 to 15	**Serving Isn't Easy**—Explore scriptures that deal with serving others.	Bibles
Bible Application	15 to 20	**Cost of Servanthood**—Complete a handout and talk about the sacrifice involved in serving others.	"Cost of Servanthood" handouts (p. 26), pencils, Bibles
Commitment	5 to 10	**Servant Fuel**—Choose a way to serve others during the coming week.	Bibles, 3×5 cards, pencils
Closing (Option 1)	up to 5	**Beyond Sacrifice**—Experience the joy of serving others.	
(Option 2)		**Serving the Servant**—Talk about ways they've been served and decide how they'll serve their partners.	

The Lesson

☐ OPTION 1: SERVING REFLECTIONS

Place a large mirror at the front of the room. Start with yourself; then have kids each stand facing the mirror while describing a time when they served someone in need. It's okay for kids to feel uncomfortable during this activity.

After kids each have described a time they served someone, form a circle.

Ask:

● **How'd you feel as you faced the mirror?** (Uncomfort-

OPENER
(5 to 10 minutes)

able; exposed; confident.)

● **Was it easy to face your reflection as you talked? Explain.** (Yes, I'm used to seeing myself in the mirror; no, I don't like the way I look.)

● **How are these feelings like the feelings people have when they serve others?** (Some people are confident servants; some people are self-conscious servants.)

Say: **Today we're going to explore some of the feelings Jesus had as a servant. And we'll see how serving can sometimes be painful or difficult.**

☐ OPTION 2: SERVANT RISKS

Form groups of no more than five. Give groups each a sheet of newsprint and a marker. Say: **Serving others often involves risks. We may risk being laughed at or ridiculed when we help an outcast. What are other risks in serving?**

Have groups each brainstorm their own list and write their ideas on their newsprint. Then have groups each read their list aloud to the rest of the class.

After the lists are read, have groups each form a circle and hold their newsprint so it becomes a flat surface. Carefully place a paper cup half-filled with water on each group's newsprint. Ask groups to walk around the room holding the cup on the newsprint—without spilling the water. After a minute, have kids form a circle.

Ask:

● **What were the risks of carrying the cup on the newsprint?** (It could spill; the newsprint could break.)

● **How is this activity like serving others?** (You don't always know what could happen when you serve others; serving others is very risky; serving others doesn't always turn out as you planned.)

Say: **Jesus is our model of servanthood. But even Jesus struggled with the pain and risks of serving. Today we'll see that while serving can be painful, we can survive the suffering. We'll learn how the joy of serving overrides the sacrifices we sometimes must make.**

Table Talk Follow-Up

If you sent the "Table Talk" handout (p. 19) to parents last week, discuss students' reactions to the activity. Ask volunteers to share what they learned from the discussion with their parents.

ACTION AND REFLECTION

(10 to 15 minutes)

SERVING ISN'T EASY

Say: **Sometimes being a servant will require tougher qualities than those we listed last week. If we look at Jesus and how people responded to his acts of service, we can begin to see the cost of servanthood.**

Ask:

● **Did Jesus put restrictions on who he'd serve? Explain.** (No, he was willing to serve everyone; yes, he only served needy people.)

Have kids kneel in a circle. If kids can't kneel (because of the way they're dressed or physical reasons), have them find a different, somewhat uncomfortable way to sit. For example, have them crouch down or sit with legs crossed. Ask different volunteers to read each of the following scripture passages: Matthew 12:9-13 and Luke 6:17-38.

For each passage, ask:

● **How could this act of service get Jesus into trouble?**
● **Who's upset in this passage?**
● **How would you feel if you were in Jesus' situation?**

After discussing the passages, ask volunteers to share times they faced conflicts because of something good they were doing. For example, someone might say, "I was put down by friends because I helped a person they didn't like" or "I got beat up because I reached out to someone who was being picked on."

Then ask:

● **How have your knees felt during this discussion?** (Uncomfortable; stiff.)

Say: **Just as we may feel uncomfortable kneeling on the floor in this discussion, we may feel uncomfortable when we serve others.**

Have kids stand up or return to their chairs.

COST OF SERVANTHOOD

Give a copy of the "Cost of Servanthood" handout (p. 26) and a pencil to each teenager. Have kids each complete their handout.

Then form groups of no more than five. Allow four minutes for kids to share their responses in their groups. Have groups discuss times they felt like the cost of serving others seemed too great.

Then ask groups each to stand in a circle. Dim the lights if possible. Read aloud 1 Corinthians 12:20-26.

Say: **Sometimes, in trying to serve the body of Christ, we experience pain. It's difficult to forget that pain and take the risk to once again serve the people who hurt us. I'm going to ask you to do something that may be hard to do. It's important that we all respect each other's feelings in this reflection time.**

One at a time, have students each enter the center of their circle and tell about a servant experience that hurt them or caused them suffering. For example, someone might tell about a time when he or she cleaned an elderly person's home even though the smell of the house made him or her sick. Remind other group members to be silent while each teenager takes a turn in the center of their circle.

BIBLE APPLICATION
(15 to 20 minutes)

When everyone has had a turn in the center, have kids sit in a large circle.

Ask:

● **How'd you feel as you told your group about a painful experience?** (Uncomfortable; scared; anxious; fine.)

● **How easy was it to tell about a painful experience? Explain.** (Not very easy, it hurts to remember; easy, I'm over it now.)

● **How would Jesus respond to the stories each person shared?** (He'd support us; he'd understand; he'd tell us he loves us.)

Say: **We all know what it's like to feel pain. Pain and suffering often are natural consequences of serving others. Yet compared to Jesus' suffering on the cross, our pain is minor. It's too easy to give up servanthood because we've been hurt or unappreciated. But it's critical that we pick up the pieces and continue to serve.**

Jesus kept serving others even when his life was at risk. He gave his life for each one of us. He wants us to continue our service to each other even though it's often a thankless job.

But we're not alone. Through the gift of the Holy Spirit, God gives us strength and endurance to serve. This same spirit was present for Jesus. Listen as I read how Isaiah describes the coming Messiah as a servant.

Have someone read aloud Isaiah 53:1-5. Have kids each think about how the feelings in the passage apply to Jesus and to their own servanthood.

Say: **Without the fuel God gives us through the Bible, each other and the Holy Spirit, serving would be too draining on us. Since we've been talking about some heavy issues today, we may be feeling a little low. As we finish today's lesson, let's take a few minutes to "refuel."**

COMMITMENT
(5 to 10 minutes)

SERVANT FUEL

Form groups of no more than four. Give Bibles, 3×5 cards and pencils to each group. Have students search through John 14—17 for passages that help boost strength when serving gets difficult. For example, John 14:1 says, "Do not let your hearts be troubled" and John 16:23 says, "My Father will give you whatever you ask in my name." Have kids write the "fuel" reminders on 3×5 cards. Then have members of each group present their cards to members of another group.

Have groups each read aloud the cards they're given. Then have teenagers each say one thing they appreciate about another person in their group that helps them feel good about serving others. For example, someone might say, "Your smile inspires me to be happy in whatever I do" or "I appreciate your dedication to serving others."

Say: **Jesus served us by dying on the cross. But now we**

can serve him by sharing his love with others.

Have groups each decide on one service action they'll take during the coming week; for example: helping fix dinner, taking a meal to a shut-in or donating time at a local soup kitchen. Have groups each tell the whole class what they're planning to do.

Encourage kids to refer to their "reminder" cards as they plan and complete their serving action.

☐ OPTION 1: BEYOND SACRIFICE

Say: **If we only think about the pain or sacrifice involved in serving, we're missing the best part. Beyond sacrifice is the incredible joy of knowing you're doing God's work in the world. And that joy makes even the most painful serving action feel good.**

Have kids stand in a circle facing in, then have them turn sideways to face right. On "go," have kids each serve each other by giving the person in front of them a back rub. After a minute, call time and close in prayer, thanking God for sending Jesus as an example of the servant lifestyle we should strive for.

☐ OPTION 2: SERVING THE SERVANT

Form pairs. Have partners each tell ways they've been served by others. For example, someone might say, "I was served when my best friend helped me with my science homework" or "I was served when my sister did my chores for me last week."

Have kids each come up with one way they can serve their partner in the coming week. Have kids each tell their partner what they'll do to serve him or her. For example, someone might say, "I'll take you out to lunch this week" or "I'll take over your household responsibilities one day this week." Have partners discuss how they'll follow through on their plans to serve one another. Then have partners pray for each other to have the strength to serve.

CLOSING
(up to 5 minutes)

If You Still Have Time . . .

Difficult Task—Form groups of no more than four. Have groups each come up with one servant project they know would be good to do but are uncomfortable about doing; for example: helping out in a nursing home, spending time with a terminally ill patient or tutoring kids with learning disabilities. Have groups each think of ways to support each other in planning and following through with their servant project.

Garden Role Play—Have students role-play the garden scene where Jesus is talking with his father (see Matthew 26:31-42). Have kids reword the dialogue to express their own feelings about being suffering servants.

COST of SERVANTHOOD

Serving as Jesus calls us to serve can be a painful and thankless job. Complete this handout to help you explore the cost of servanthood.

● Think of a time you did something for people and they didn't appreciate your efforts. Write a brief description of what you did for them.

● List the positive feelings or actions you experienced when you first had the idea to provide your service.

● List the negative feelings or actions you experienced while serving in this role.

● What'd you decide to do the next time this opportunity to serve came up?

● What do you think Jesus would've said or done in this situation?

● If appreciation for work done isn't the reason to serve, what is?

SERVING FAMILY AND FRIENDS

LESSON 3

Sometimes, when teenagers think about what it means to be a servant, they only think of mission work or serving people in other parts of the world. But Jesus taught us to serve those close to us too. Teenagers need to realize that servanthood starts at home and with friends.

To help senior highers discover ways to serve family and friends.

Students will:
- talk about how it feels to be served;
- serve each other;
- list ways they can serve family and friends; and
- commit to completing a service project in the coming week.

Look up the following scriptures. Then read the background paragraphs to see how the passages relate to your senior highers.

In **John 13:3-6**, Jesus washes the disciples' feet.

In Jesus' time, people wore sandals in the dusty streets. Foot-washing was a regular occurrence—but was usually done by servants of the house. In this dramatic scene, Jesus taught a lesson in humility for his disciples to see.

Teenagers feel uncomfortable about doing things that might make them look "stupid." But sometimes, serving is like that. By reading this scripture, teenagers can see the importance of becoming a servant—no matter how others might perceive them.

In **1 John 3:17-18**, John challenges Christians to love in deed and truth.

LESSON AIM

OBJECTIVES

BIBLE BASIS
JOHN 13:3-6
1 JOHN 3:17-18

This passage stresses the importance of *doing* things for other people, not just *talking* about doing them. Verse 18 supports the common phrase "actions speak louder than words."

Our society is acutely aware of problems in the world. But much of the concern voiced by people is nothing more than lip service. Teenagers need to understand that serving others isn't accomplished through discussion or concern—but action. These verses can remind kids to love friends and family with actions.

THIS LESSON AT A GLANCE

Section	Minutes	What Students Will Do	Supplies
Opener (Option 1)	5 to 10	**May I Serve You?**—Experience what it's like to be served.	Room decorations (optional), doughnuts or cookies, juice
(Option 2)		**Service, Please**—Enjoy being served by volunteers.	Breakfast foods or snacks
Action and Reflection	15 to 20	**Joyful Serving**—Experience serving and being served.	Pitcher of cold water, cups, "Serving Menu" handouts (p. 33)
Bible Application	10 to 15	**Unexpected Service**—Explore Jesus' example of service and wash each other's feet (or hands).	Bibles, large bowls or basins, water, towels, music (optional)
Commitment	5 to 10	**Serving Ways**—Brainstorm ways to serve family members and friends.	Tape, newsprint, marker, 3×5 cards, pencils
Closing (Option 1)	up to 5	**Circle of Servants**—Pass a towel around a circle and say how they feel as servants.	Towel from Unexpected Service
(Option 2)		**Secret Servants**—Commit to serve each other during the week.	Paper slips, pencils, box

The Lesson

☐ OPTION 1: MAY I SERVE YOU?

Before the Lesson

If possible, decorate the room like a restaurant. Place tablecloths on the tables, and be sure lots of comfortable chairs are available.

As students enter the room, ask them to make themselves comfortable. Go around the room and serve kids some kind of refreshment, such as doughnuts or cookies, and juice.

Go out of your way to talk with each teenager and provide for his or her needs.

After a few minutes of serving the kids, ask:

● **How'd it feel to be served as you came into class?** (Strange; warm; fun.)

● **What made my serving you special or unusual?** (It was unexpected; you made me feel welcome.)

● **Not counting my service to you right now, what was the last thing someone did to serve you?** (My friend helped me with my homework; my dad let me borrow the car; my mom made me a great lunch.)

Say: **Think about the last time you served someone else. Think about who you served and what you did. Just as you probably enjoyed the unexpected service I gave you, your friends and family enjoy it when you surprise them with a serving act. Today we're going to discover ways to serve friends and family.**

☐ OPTION 2: SERVICE, PLEASE

Place breakfast foods or snacks on a table in the room. Form groups of no more than five. Ask for one volunteer from each group to be that group's "Servant." Have members of each group give instructions to their Servants such as "get me a drink of water," "scratch my back" or "get me something to eat." Tell groups to give Servants lots of requests at once. Have Servants each try to comply with the requests from their group members.

After one minute, call "switch" and have a new volunteer from each group serve in place of the original Servant for that group. After two or three volunteers have each served their group, call time.

Ask the Servants:

● **How'd you feel as you tried to serve the people in your group?** (Frustrated; confused; angry.)

● **How is serving others when they expect to be served different from serving others unexpectedly?** (Expected serving isn't as fun; unexpected service is more fulfilling.)

Say: **Just as you were served by the volunteers in your group, you can serve your friends and family. But even more, we can learn to give unexpected service to people who are close to us.**

JOYFUL SERVING

Place a pitcher of cold water and a bunch of cups at the front of the room. Form pairs, and have one volunteer from each pair get a copy of the "Serving Menu" handout (p. 33).
Tell volunteers to each serve their partner according to the instructions on the handout. Tell volunteers not to say what they're doing or why.

After volunteers each have completed their servant task, form a circle.

Ask the volunteer servants:

● **How'd it feel to serve your partner?** (Great; embarrassing; uncomfortable.)

● **Is it easy to serve others? Why or why not?** (No, people are too uncomfortable or embarrassed when you help them; yes, I enjoy doing things for others; no, it's embarrassing for me.)

Ask the partners who were served:

● **How'd you feel when you were being served? Explain.** (Nervous, I didn't know what to expect; fine, I enjoyed being waited on.)

Ask everyone:

● **What are the positive results of serving others?** (The people served enjoy it; the servants feel good; God smiles on your work.)

Say: **In this experience, some of you got to serve your friends. Serving friends and family is an important part of our faith. Let's take a look at what the Bible says about serving each other.**

UNEXPECTED SERVICE

Have a volunteer read aloud John 13:3-6.

Ask:

● **Why do you think the apostles had such a difficult time accepting the service Jesus had to offer them?** (He was their teacher; they felt they should be serving him; they felt unworthy to receive this service; it was unexpected.)

Say: **This kind of service can be very humbling. Those of you who were servants in the last activity, form a circle with your chairs and sit down. Those of you who were served, sit in front of the person who served you. I'm go-**

ACTION AND REFLECTION

(15 to 20 minutes)

BIBLE APPLICATION

(10 to 15 minutes)

ing to pass around a basin and towels. Like Jesus, gently wash the feet of your servant. (If girls in your class are wearing nylons, have kids gently wash the girls' hands instead.) As you serve, thank your partner for the service he or she provided. Then name the servant qualities you most admire in your partner, such as kindness, patience or humility.

Play quiet reflective music to set a prayerful atmosphere. Remind kids to be serious during this activity. During this time, read aloud 1 John 3:17-18.

After the activity, ask the original servants:
● **How'd you feel about having your feet washed? Explain.** (Uncomfortable, I was embarrassed; humble, I didn't feel I deserved to be served.)
● **How'd you feel being served by the people who you'd served earlier?** (It was neat; I enjoyed it; I was surprised.)
● **How can Jesus' example of servanthood help us be better servants to our friends and family?** (His example reminds us we can serve anyone; his example helps us understand that no one is too good to be a servant.)

Say: **Foot-washing may not be the best way for you to serve your friends or family on a daily basis, but it's important to find ways to serve—especially unexpected ways.**

SERVING WAYS

Tape a sheet of newsprint to the wall. Have kids brainstorm ways to serve their friends and family members. Write these on the newsprint. Encourage kids to be creative. For example, someone might say, "Cook a meal for your family," "Do a friend's chores for a day" or "Organize your family photos."

Give a 3×5 card and a pencil to each student. Have kids each choose one idea from the list to do during the week. Have them each write their idea and name on their 3×5 card. Collect the cards. Say: **Next week, we'll briefly review the cards to see how you did following through on your plan to serve.**

Hang on to the cards until next week.

☐ OPTION 1: CIRCLE OF SERVANTS

Form a circle. Pass a towel from the Unexpected Service activity around the circle. As kids each hold the towel, have them say one word that describes how they feel as servants. For example, someone might say, "Thankful," "Overwhelmed" or "Joyful." After everyone's spoken, close with a moment of silent prayer. Remind kids to follow through with their plan to serve a family member or friend in the coming week.

COMMITMENT
(5 to 10 minutes)

CLOSING
(up to 5 minutes)

☐ OPTION 2: SECRET SERVANTS

Give kids each a paper slip and a pencil. Have kids each write their name on their paper. Then place the papers in a box and mix them up. Pass the box around the room, and have kids each take one slip. Be sure kids don't get their own name. Say: **During the coming week, serve the person whose name is on your paper in at least three different ways. These could include praying, helping with home-work or doing an errand.**

Tell kids not to tell whose name they have. Close by thanking God for the gift of friends and family, and the ability to serve them.

If You Still Have Time . . .

Serving Thoughts—Have students tell about times they felt lonely, imprisoned or hungry. For example, someone might say, "I felt lonely my first day of school" or "I felt imprisoned when my parents got a divorce." Discuss how people can serve each other during these times.

Servant Skits—Form teams. Have teams each come up with three ways people serve each other. Then have teams silently act out these servant roles for the other teams to guess. After teams each guess the servant activity, talk briefly about the variety of ways people can serve each other.

*D*uring the next few minutes, you'll be serving your partner in a number of different ways. Don't tell him or her what you'll be doing or why. Just follow the "courses" one at a time. When you're done, sit quietly next to your partner.

Serving Menu

Course One:

Make your partner comfortable by giving him or her a back rub that lasts no less than one minute.

Course Two:

Take off your partner's shoes, and give him or her a nice foot massage. Remember, no comments about smelly feet. This is a time to be serious.

Course Three:

Tell your partner three things you really appreciate about him or her. For example, you might say, "You're a great leader" or "I appreciate your ability to say what you feel in class." Be sincere and positive.

Course Four:

Get a cup of water for your partner. The supplies are available in this room.

Course Five:

Find out at least one concern your partner has that you can pray for. Then offer a brief prayer for your partner.

LESSON 4

SERVING THE WORLD

S ome of the world's problems seem too big to do anything about. Teenagers just don't think their "two cents' worth" will make much difference. But Jesus calls us to serve the world. Teenagers can learn to serve the world, one small piece at a time.

LESSON AIM

To help senior highers find ways to serve their neighbors around the world.

OBJECTIVES

Students will:
● discover who their neighbors are;
● experience reaching out to others;
● brainstorm ways to serve people they don't usually serve; and
● plan and commit to do a service project in the coming weeks.

BIBLE BASIS
LUKE 9:10-17
LUKE 10:25-37

Look up the following scriptures. Then read the background paragraphs to see how the passages relate to your senior highers.

In **Luke 9:10-17**, Jesus feeds the 5,000.

In this familiar story, Jesus performs a miracle by feeding many people with only a little food. While it's easy to focus on the wonder of this event, the real message seems to be not *how* but *that* Jesus served the multitudes. His close relationship with God gave him the knowledge and ability to reach out to people in need.

Teenagers might read this scripture passage and say, "Wow, that's great." But they need to see beyond the miracle to the message. Many of the world's problems may seem insurmountable. But with God's help, we can learn to reach out to people in need—just as Jesus did.

In **Luke 10:25-37**, Jesus tells the parable of the Good Samaritan.

Samaritans were despised by Jews because they had a mixed heritage and different worship. Jesus' point in this parable wasn't to defame the Levites or priests. His message was that we should ignore cultural or ethnic boundaries and show mercy to all people.

Teenagers have their own "Levites," "priests" and "Samaritans." Sometimes kids may refuse to help people because they don't want to get involved. This passage reminds teenagers to be like the Samaritan and reach out to all people.

THIS LESSON AT A GLANCE

Section	Minutes	What Students Will Do	Supplies
Opener (Option 1)	5 to 10	**What in the World?**—Play a game and brainstorm ways to serve the world.	Cards from the Serving Ways activity in Lesson 3, large plastic ball, permanent markers
(Option 2)		**Flip Side**—Think about ways they can help people they don't know.	Cards from Serving Ways activity in Lesson 3, 3×5 cards, pencils
Bible Application	10 to 15	**Who Is My Neighbor?**—Perform skits and discover Jesus' definition of "neighbor."	Bibles, "New Parables" handouts (p. 40)
Action and Reflection	10 to 15	**Creative Servanthood**—Experience serving each other in creative ways.	Cup, towel, pencil, paper, bowl of water, string, tape
Commitment	10 to 15	**Go Out and Do It**—Plan a service project to begin working on as a group.	"Serving Plan" handouts (p. 41), pencils
Closing (Option 1)	up to 5	**Commission**—Participate in a moment of worship and think about their commission to help others.	Bible, loaf of bread
(Option 2)		**Servant Prayers**—Pray for patience and servant-like attitudes.	

The Lesson

☐ OPTION 1: WHAT IN THE WORLD?

Give kids their cards from the Serving Ways activity from Lesson 3. If you have new students this week, tell them what the activity was about. Then ask kids each to think about

OPENER
(5 to 10 minutes)

how well they completed the task written on their card. Encourage kids to tell how they felt if they did or didn't complete the servant project for family or friends.

Form two teams, and have them each form a circle. Give each team a large plastic ball at least 12 inches in diameter (a beach ball or sturdy balloon will work). Give kids each a permanent marker.

Say: **This ball represents the world. On "go," begin tossing the ball around your circle. When you catch the ball, you must write on the ball one way you can serve the world. For example, you could write, "Feed the hungry." You may not throw the ball to another person until you write one idea that's not been used yet. Teammates may help each other brainstorm ideas.**

Allow three minutes for teams to pass the balls around. Then have volunteers read the ideas on each ball.

Ask:

● **How'd you feel as you tried to quickly think of something to write?** (Nervous; uncomfortable; fine.)

● **How'd you feel about the help you got from friends?** (I appreciated their ideas; they helped me think of something to write.)

Say: **When we think about serving the world, we may feel uncomfortable. But just as you helped your teammates come up with ideas in this game, you can help each other discover ways to serve others. That's our goal for today's lesson.**

☐ OPTION 2: FLIP SIDE

Give kids their cards from the Serving Ways activity from Lesson 3. If you have new students this week, tell them what the activity was about. Give new students each a blank 3×5 card. Then ask kids each to think about how well they completed the task written on their card. Encourage kids to tell how they felt if they did or didn't complete the servant project for family or friends.

Give kids each a pencil. Say: **On the back of your card, write one way you can serve people you don't know. For example, you might write, "I can spend time at a local soup kitchen" or "I can raise money to help fight hunger in other countries."**

Form pairs. Have partners each tell what they wrote and answer the following questions:

● **How easy was it to think of something to do for people you don't know?**

● **Is it easier or harder to serve people outside your family and circle of friends? Explain.**

Say: **Last week we learned the importance of serving people we know well. This week we'll examine how Jesus' call to serve involves people we don't know.**

WHO IS MY NEIGHBOR?

Ask:

● **Who's your neighbor?** (Everyone; people we come in contact with.)

Say: **Let's take a look at a familiar story from the Bible that helps us understand who our neighbors are.**

Assign the following roles: Lawyer, Jesus, robbers, priest, Levite, Samaritan, innkeeper and injured man. If you have a small class, have people play more than one role. If you have a large class, have more than one set of actors. Be sure each person in the class has a part. Read aloud Luke 10:25-37 while the characters act out the story. Pause as necessary for characters to act.

When you've read the story, ask:

● **Why did Jesus tell this parable?** (To remind people to care for each other; to help people know who their neighbors are.)

● **Based on this parable, how should we respond to people in need?** (We need to take care of them; we should reach out to them.)

Say: **The parable we just read can be updated to our time too.**

Form groups of no more than six. Give groups each a copy of the "New Parables" handout (p. 40). Have groups each choose one situation to act out. Tell kids they may speak in their skits, but that the skits must not take longer than one minute—or less, depending on the number of groups. You might want to assign situations so there won't be duplication.

Have groups each present their skit. Then ask:

● **What do each of these skits tell us about serving others?** (We need to do what we can for people in need; serving others is part of our growth as Christians.)

● **How is Jesus' parable relevant today?** (We need to help people who are in need; we need to be like the Samaritan.)

Say: **Jesus' parable was written for you and me. And we can act on that parable today by serving people in need.**

CREATIVE SERVANTHOOD

Say: **The man in Jesus' parable was willing to serve his neighbor. This example of unexpected service opens our eyes to a group of people we're called to serve—the outcast, the despised, the needy and the hopeless.**

Ask:

● **Why do some people have a hard time serving these people?** (Some people don't think they can help others; some people don't see the problems, so they don't act; they're afraid to get involved.)

Form a circle. In the center of the circle, place the following items: an empty cup, a towel, a pencil, a sheet of paper, a bowl of water, a piece of string, and a roll of tape. Say: **For**

BIBLE APPLICATION
(10 to 15 minutes)

ACTION AND REFLECTION
(10 to 15 minutes)

the next few minutes, we're going to try a serving experiment. One at a time, take one item from the center of the circle and use it to serve one or more people in this room. For example, you may pick up the towel and go wipe someone's forehead or hands.

No one may talk during this exercise. You may not use an object the same way someone else uses it. Don't take longer than 15 to 30 seconds during your turn.

Starting with the person on your left, have kids go around the circle serving each other. Remind kids to be silent and choose actions that are positive.

After each person has had his or her turn serving, ask:

● **How'd you feel as you tried to think of creative ways to serve?** (It was fun; I was nervous; I didn't know what to do.)

● **How is that like the feeling people have when they serve others they don't know?** (Some people don't feel comfortable serving others; some people enjoy serving others.)

Say: **In this exercise, we had to be creative in our approach to serving. We can't solve hunger by sending our leftovers to the hungry people. Nor can we solve poverty by giving everyone a credit card. Creativity is important when serving others.**

COMMITMENT
(10 to 15 minutes)

GO OUT AND DO IT

Give kids each a copy of the "Serving Plan" handout (p. 41) and a pencil. Form groups of no more than four. Allow five minutes for groups to brainstorm service projects they can do for people they don't know; for example: feeding the homeless, raising money to send to charities, sponsoring a child through Compassion International, Box 7000, Colorado Springs, CO 80933.

Have groups complete a handout for each idea. Then have groups each present their ideas to the whole class. Have class members discuss which idea or ideas can be implemented right away. Have the teenagers vote on the project(s) they want to commit to during the week. Then ask for volunteers to head up the project. Encourage kids to each commit to becoming involved in the project.

During the coming week, help the project leaders follow through with the plan.

Say: **Our commitment to this project is one way we can commit to serving others. But we can also commit to a life of service that goes beyond any projects we plan. Some of you may even want to commit to a life of serving people as missionaries in another culture.**

Form pairs. Have partners share how they feel about what it means to live a life of service. Ask them to talk about how they'd feel as missionaries in a foreign land.

Say: **Serving others requires many skills—including**

patience, love, kindness and concern. Each of you has one or more of these skills.

Have kids each tell their partner skills and characteristics that make him or her a good servant. Remind kids to be positive and sincere.

☐ OPTION 1: COMMISSION

Read aloud Luke 9:10-17. At the end of the story, say: **Jesus fed the people who came to listen to his message because they were hungry and had long journeys ahead of them. We too have a task before us—and a great journey of service to pursue.**

Pick up a large loaf of bread, and have each student come up and break off a piece to eat. When kids each have a piece of bread, say: **Jesus has called us to serve the world. With this bread, let us gain strength to go out and serve.**

Have kids each eat their piece of bread and pray silently. Close by saying aloud: **Amen**.

☐ OPTION 2: SERVANT PRAYERS

Have group members link arms in a circle. Have kids each offer prayers for the servant project(s) they plan to complete in the coming weeks. Have them pray for God's strength and power to give everyone in the group patience and servant-like attitudes. Close with a group hug. Thank kids for committing to follow Jesus' example of servanthood.

If You Still Have Time . . .

Servant Charades—Have kids play a game of Guess the Servant. Have kids each take a turn pantomiming famous biblical servants such as Moses, Jesus, Mary and Martha, and Peter. Have the group try to guess the servants and briefly discuss the qualities each servant possessed.

Course Reflection—Form a circle. Ask students to reflect on the past four lessons. Have them take turns completing the following sentences:
- Something I learned in this course was . . .
- If I could tell my friends about this course, I'd say . . .
- Something I'll do differently because of this course is . . .

NEW PARABLES

Situation 1: Sandy is concerned about the homeless problem in her town. She gathers a few friends together and visits the people on the streets. In your skit, show what Sandy and her friends do to serve the homeless people.

Situation 2: Mike wants to help fight hunger. He goes to a friend's house to talk about what he can do, but his friend says he can't make a dent in the problem—so "why bother?" In your skit, show how Mike responds to his friend's lack of confidence.

Situation 3: Lexi and Gene are out walking one evening when they notice a drunk—barely alive—lying by the side of the road. In your skit, show the conversation Lexi and Gene have as they talk about whether to help the drunk and what to do.

Situation 4: Jeri, Dan and Melissa just started their spring vacation. They've been planning a week of relaxation and fun. Bob comes in with news of a tornado that just tore apart a town only 50 miles away. Bob thinks they should all go help clean up the town. Dan and Melissa have doubts about getting involved. In your skit, show the reactions to Bob's request and the discussion that follows.

Project Description:

- What's the project?

- Who will the project serve?

- What needs will we meet?

- Who'll be involved in the project?

Project Plan:

- Who do we need to contact before doing this project?

- Do we need any special permission? Explain.

- How long will the project take to complete?

- How much money will the project require?

- How'll the money be raised for this project?

- When will we start this project?

SERVING PLAN

BONUS IDEAS

Real Servants in Action—Invite someone who's served in your community in a difficult role; for example: a hospice worker, a family counselor or someone who's worked with AIDS patients. Have your guest talk about the joys and heart-aches of serving.

Servant Thanks—Have kids write thank-you notes to people in the church who serve as volunteers; for example: greeters, choir members, Sunday school teachers and babysitters. In their letters, have kids tell the volunteers they appreciate the service they share with the church.

Rub Me the Right Way—After your church service, have group members set up a "Free Back Rubs" station near the entrance to the church. Encourage people to sit and receive free back rubs from the teenagers. Have teenagers give each person who accepts the service a card with "Thanks for letting the teenagers of your church rub you the right way" written on it. *Don't* make this a fund-raiser. Kids will learn more about serving others if this is done as a free service for the church.

Serving With Style Newsletter Insert—Have teenagers in-terview people in your church who are good servants. Have kids write short articles based on these interviews and pub-lish them in your church or youth newsletter. If possible, include a photograph of the person interviewed. Congratulate the "Super Servant" of the week during the church service.

Serving Together—Have kids and their parents plan a ser-vant project to work on together, such as serving a meal to the homeless or raising money to help fight hunger. After completing the project, have parents and kids enjoy a dinner together and celebrate the joy of serving.

If I Were a Rich Person—Play the song "If I Were a Rich Man" from *Fiddler on the Roof*. Give kids each $200 in play money. Then ask them how they'd spend the money to help serve others. For example, someone might buy shoes and socks for a poor family. Have catalogs available so kids can gauge their expenditures accurately. Consider ways to collect money to help people in need.

Missionary Encouragement—Have kids write notes of en-couragement to people doing local or international missionary

MEETINGS AND MORE

work for your church. Have kids tell the missionaries they appreciate their examples of servanthood.

Could I Be a Missionary?—Invite people in all sorts of roles to share how they're servants on their jobs. For example, have a mom, a missionary, a computer programmer, an artist and a maintenance worker from your church visit with kids about their "mission" fields. Help kids see how they can be servants in many different roles.

Family Servant Coupons—Copy and distribute the "Family Servant Coupons" handout (p. 46). Have kids each fill in six coupons, cut them apart and staple them to form a booklet to give to their parents. Have kids report back to the class about how the coupons worked and how they felt serving their families.

Workcamp Opportunity—Consider giving your kids a chance to serve others by taking them to a workcamp. Get information about Group's workcamps by writing to Group Workcamps, Box 481, Loveland, CO 80539.

Table Talk—Use the "Table Talk" handout (p. 19) as the basis for a meeting with parents and teenagers. During the meeting, have parents and kids complete the handout and discuss it. Include activities where parents serve their kids and kids serve their parents. Use ideas from *Quick Crowdbreakers and Games for Youth Groups* (Group Books) to get the meeting going.

PARTY PLEASERS

Serving-the-World Party—Plan a party on the theme of serving the world. Have kids each collect donations for a world service charity such as an entry ticket to the party. Consider charities such as Church World Service, Box 968, Elkhart, IN 46515; World Vision 919 W. Huntington Dr., Monrovia, CA 91016; or contact your denomination for other recommendations. During the party, play volleyball with a beach ball painted to look like a globe. Serve foods representing various countries. Play music from all around the world. During the party, have kids plan a service project to work on.

Service Reversal—Have kids identify a number of people in your community who are servants; for example: volunteers at church, waitresses, people who do volunteer work in the community. Have kids invite these people to a meal. Have kids prepare a meal and serve the guests. Also have kids briefly talk about Jesus' example of servanthood.

Serving Each Other—Plan a retreat with the theme of serving each other. Include activities where kids serve each other in different ways. For example, have kids prepare a meal for the rest of the group; have kids give back rubs during discussion times; have kids prepare meeting rooms when needed; or have kids take turns serving a partner by getting him or her snacks.

Use the following scriptures as a starting point for your discussion times: Matthew 5:41-42; Mark 8:34; Romans 15:1-2; James 2:14-18; and 1 John 3:17-18.

Have kids create a worship service to close the retreat that focuses on the importance of following Jesus' example of servanthood.

RETREAT IDEA

FAMILY SERVANT COUPONS

SERVANT COUPON

To_____

This coupon is good for one act of service from me to you. The act of service is described below.

I will_____

_____

This coupon is good until you use it. No expiration date. I hereby signify by my signature that this is an official Servant Coupon. Accept no substitutes.

Signed: _____

SERVANT COUPON

To_____

This coupon is good for one act of service from me to you. The act of service is described below.

I will_____

_____

This coupon is good until you use it. No expiration date. I hereby signify by my signature that this is an official Servant Coupon. Accept no substitutes.

Signed: _____

SERVANT COUPON

To_____

This coupon is good for one act of service from me to you. The act of service is described below.

I will_____

_____

This coupon is good until you use it. No expiration date. I hereby signify by my signature that this is an official Servant Coupon. Accept no substitutes.

Signed: _____

CURRICULUM REORDER—TOP PRIORITY

 Order now to prepare for your upcoming Sunday school classes, youth ministry meetings, and weekend retreats! Each book includes all teacher and student materials—plus photocopiable handouts—for any size class . . . for just $8.99 each!

FOR SENIOR HIGH:

1 & 2 Corinthians: Christian Discipleship, ISBN 1-55945-230-7

Angels, Demons, Miracles & Prayer, ISBN 1-55945-235-8

Changing the World, ISBN 1-55945-236-6

Christians in a Non-Christian World, ISBN 1-55945-224-2

Christlike Leadership, ISBN 1-55945-231-5

Communicating With Friends, ISBN 1-55945-228-5

Counterfeit Religions, ISBN 1-55945-207-2

Dating Decisions, ISBN 1-55945-215-3

Dealing With Life's Pressures, ISBN 1-55945-232-3

Deciphering Jesus' Parables, ISBN 1-55945-237-4

Exodus: Following God, ISBN 1-55945-226-9

Exploring Ethical Issues, ISBN 1-55945-225-0

Faith for Tough Times, ISBN 1-55945-216-1

Forgiveness, ISBN 1-55945-223-4

Getting Along With Parents, ISBN 1-55945-202-1

Getting Along With Your Family, ISBN 1-55945-233-1

The Gospel of John: Jesus' Teachings, ISBN 1-55945-208-0

Hazardous to Your Health: AIDS, Steroids & Eating Disorders, ISBN 1-55945-200-5

Is Marriage in Your Future?, ISBN 1-55945-203-X

Jesus' Death & Resurrection, ISBN 1-55945-211-0

The Joy of Serving, ISBN 1-55945-210-2

Knowing God's Will, ISBN 1-55945-205-6

Life After High School, ISBN 1-55945-220-X

Making Good Decisions, ISBN 1-55945-209-9

Money: A Christian Perspective, ISBN 1-55945-212-9

Movies, Music, TV & Me, ISBN 1-55945-213-7

Overcoming Insecurities, ISBN 1-55945-221-8

Psalms, ISBN 1-55945-234-X

Responding to Injustice, ISBN 1-55945-214-5

Revelation, ISBN 1-55945-229-3

School Struggles, ISBN 1-55945-201-3

Sex: A Christian Perspective, ISBN 1-55945-206-4

Today's Lessons From Yesterday's Prophets, ISBN 1-55945-227-7

Turning Depression Upside Down, ISBN 1-55945-135-1

What Is the Church?, ISBN 1-55945-222-6

Who Is God?, ISBN 1-55945-218-8

Who Is Jesus?, ISBN 1-55945-219-6

Who Is the Holy Spirit?, ISBN 1-55945-217-X

Your Life as a Disciple, ISBN 1-55945-204-8

FOR JUNIOR HIGH/MIDDLE SCHOOL:

Accepting Others: Beyond Barriers & Stereotypes, ISBN 1-55945-126-2

Advice to Young Christians: Exploring Paul's Letters, ISBN 1-55945-146-7

Applying the Bible to Life, ISBN 1-55945-116-5

Becoming Responsible, ISBN 1-55945-109-2

Bible Heroes: Joseph, Esther, Mary & Peter, ISBN 1-55945-137-8

Boosting Self-Esteem, ISBN 1-55945-100-9

Building Better Friendships, ISBN 1-55945-138-6

Can Christians Have Fun?, ISBN 1-55945-134-3

Caring for God's Creation, ISBN 1-55945-121-1

Christmas: A Fresh Look, ISBN 1-55945-124-6

Competition, ISBN 1-55945-133-5

Dealing With Death, ISBN 1-55945-112-2

Dealing With Disappointment, ISBN 1-55945-139-4

Doing Your Best, ISBN 1-55945-142-4

Drugs & Drinking, ISBN 1-55945-118-1

Evil and the Occult, ISBN 1-55945-102-5

Genesis: The Beginnings, ISBN 1-55945-111-4

Guys & Girls: Understanding Each Other, ISBN 1-55945-110-6

Handling Conflict, ISBN 1-55945-125-4

Heaven & Hell, ISBN 1-55945-131-9

Is God Unfair?, ISBN 1-55945-108-4

Love or Infatuation?, ISBN 1-55945-128-9

Making Parents Proud, ISBN 1-55945-107-6

Making the Most of School, ISBN 1-55945-113-0

Materialism, ISBN 1-55945-130-0

The Miracle of Easter, ISBN 1-55945-143-2

Miracles!, ISBN 1-55945-117-3

Peace & War, ISBN 1-55945-123-8

Peer Pressure, ISBN 1-55945-103-3

Prayer, ISBN 1-55945-104-1

Reaching Out to a Hurting World, ISBN 1-55945-140-8

Sermon on the Mount, ISBN 1-55945-129-7

Suicide: The Silent Epidemic, ISBN 1-55945-145-9

Telling Your Friends About Christ, ISBN 1-55945-114-9

The Ten Commandments, ISBN 1-55945-127-0

Today's Media: Choosing Wisely, ISBN 1-55945-144-0

Today's Music: Good or Bad?, ISBN 1-55945-101-7

What Is God's Purpose for Me?, ISBN 1-55945-132-7

What's a Christian?, ISBN 1-55945-105-X

Order today from your local Christian bookstore, or write: Group Publishing, Box 485, Loveland, CO 80539. For mail orders, please add postage/handling of $4 for orders up to $15, $5 for orders of $15.01+. Colorado residents add 3% sales tax.

BRING THE BIBLE TO LIFE FOR YOUR 5TH- AND 6TH-GRADERS WITH GROUP'S *HANDS-ON BIBLE CURRICULUM*™

Energize your kids with Active Learning!

Group's **Hands-On Bible Curriculum**™ will help you teach the Bible in a radical new way. It's based on Active Learning—the same teaching method Jesus used.

Research shows that we retain less than 10% of what we hear or read. *But we remember up to 90% of what we experience.* Your 5th- and 6th-graders will experience spiritual lessons and learn to apply them to their daily lives! And—they'll go home remembering what they've learned.

In each lesson, students will participate in exciting and memorable learning experiences using fascinating gadgets and gizmos you've not seen with any other curriculum. Your 5th- and 6th-graders will discover biblical truths and <u>remember</u> what they learn—because they're <u>doing</u> instead of just listening.

You'll save time and money too!

While students are learning more, you'll be working less—simply follow the quick and easy instructions in the Teachers Guide. You'll get tons of material for an energy-packed 35- to 60-minute lesson. And, if you have extra time, there's an arsenal of Bonus Ideas and Time Stuffers to keep kids occupied—and learning! Plus, you'll SAVE BIG over other curriculum programs that require you to buy expensive separate student books—all student handouts in Group's Hands-On Bible Curriculum™ are photocopiable!

In addition to the easy-to-use Teachers Guide, you'll get all the essential teaching materials you need in a ready-to-use Learning Lab™. No more running from store to store hunting for lesson materials—all the active-learning tools you need to teach 13 exciting Bible lessons to any size class are provided for you in the Learning Lab™.

Challenging topics every 13 weeks keep your kids coming back!

Group's Hands-On Bible Curriculum™ covers topics that matter to your kids and teaches them the Bible with integrity. Every quarter you'll explore 3 meaningful Bible-based subjects. Switching topics every month keeps your 5th- and 6th-graders enthused and coming back for more. The full 2-year program will help your kids...

- make God-pleasing decisions,
- recognize their God-given potential, and
- seek to grow as Christians.

Take the boredom out of Sunday school, children's church, and youth group for your 5th- and 6th-graders. Make your job easier and more rewarding with no-fail lessons that are ready in a flash. Order Group's Hands-On Bible Curriculum™ for your 5th- and 6th-graders today.

Order today from your local Christian bookstore, or write: Group Publishing, Box 485, Loveland, CO 80539. For mail orders, please add postage/handling of $4 for orders up to $15, $5 for orders of $15.01+. Colorado residents add 3% sales tax.